WHY CRYPTO - BDX DREAMS

ENTRY LEVEL UNDERSTANDINGS OF HOW CRYPTO CAN HELP YOU ACHEIVE YOUR DREAMS

JITHENDER KUMAR R

Made with ♥ on the Notion Press Platform
www.notionpress.com

To all the Dreamcatchers,

This book is dedicated to all the dreamers who dare to envision a brighter future for themselves and their loved ones. To the curious minds exploring uncharted territories, and to those who inspire me daily with their resilience, determination, and unwavering belief in possibilities.

Your support and encouragement have been the cornerstone of this journey. May this book serve as a guide and a reminder that with knowledge and courage, dreams are within reach.

Contents

Foreword *vii*

Preface *ix*

Acknowledgements *xi*

Prologue *xiii*

1. Chapter 1: The Crypto Revolution 1
2. Chapter 2: Crypto Basics For Beginners 5
3. Chapter 3: Why Crypto Matters For Indians 9
4. Chapter 4: Decoding Crypto Investments 18
5. Chapter 5: Getting Started With Crypto 27
6. Chapter 6: Making Crypto Work For You 35
7. Chapter 7: Crypto As A Tool To Achieve Dreams 43
8. Chapter 8: Challenges And Myths About Crypto 52
9. Chapter 9: The Future Of Crypto In India 60
10. Chapter 10: Your Crypto Journey Starts Here 69
11. Chapter 11: Importance Of KYC In The Cryptocurrency World 76
12. Reader's Summary 85

Gratitude 87

FOREWORD

In an era where technology is redefining how we live, work, and interact, cryptocurrency has emerged as a game-changer—a disruptive force poised to reshape the global economy. For many, however, the world of crypto feels shrouded in complexity, reserved for tech-savvy enthusiasts or financial experts. But the truth is, cryptocurrency is for everyone.

Why Crypto is a timely guide for anyone curious about stepping into this fascinating world. Designed with simplicity and clarity in mind, this book demystifies cryptocurrency for beginners, especially Indian working professionals, freelancers, and dreamers who aspire to achieve financial independence. It speaks directly to those who yearn for growth but don't know where to start and introduces the tools to harness crypto to achieve their dreams.

Through its thoughtfully crafted chapters, Why Crypto takes you on a journey—from understanding the basics of cryptocurrency to exploring its real-world applications and potential as a passive income source. The book delves into the nuances of setting up wallets, trading, and investing, while also shedding light on the risks, legal implications, and future trends of this ever-evolving domain.

As you turn these pages, you will not only gain knowledge but also a renewed sense of empowerment to take control of your financial future. The author's approach—grounded in practical insights and tailored for an Indian audience—ensures that even the most novice reader can grasp the concepts and feel inspired to begin their crypto journey.

Whether you are a seasoned professional looking to diversify your income streams or someone with big dreams but no clear path to achieving them, this book is your starting point. Let it guide you, educate you, and motivate you to explore the boundless opportunities that cryptocurrency offers.

Welcome to the world of crypto. Your journey begins here.

JAMIL JACKISYING, Business Owner

Preface

Cryptocurrency is no longer just a buzzword; it's a phenomenon that has revolutionized the way we perceive money, investments, and financial independence. Yet, for many, the idea of stepping into the crypto world remains daunting. Questions like "Where do I start?", "Is it safe?", or "Can it really help me achieve my dreams?" often deter potential explorers from taking the first step.

This book, Why Crypto, was born out of a simple idea: to bridge the gap between curiosity and confidence for those new to cryptocurrency. As someone who has witnessed both the skepticism and the transformative potential of crypto, I felt compelled to create a resource that could simplify this complex world and make it accessible to everyone—especially to Indian professionals, freelancers, and anyone eager to unlock new opportunities for growth and financial freedom.

Through its pages, Why Crypto takes you on a journey, starting from the very basics of understanding cryptocurrency and blockchain technology to more practical aspects like setting up wallets, investing, and navigating risks. It also explores real-life applications, future trends, and how crypto can play a vital role in achieving your dreams.

This book is not a get-rich-quick manual or a technical deep dive. Instead, it is a guide for the uninitiated, written with the intent to empower and inspire. It's for those who want to take control of their financial destiny but don't know where to begin. It's for the dreamers who believe in the power of innovation and are ready to embrace the future.

As you read through the chapters, my hope is that you will not only understand cryptocurrency but also feel equipped to take the first steps into this dynamic and promising world. Remember, every expert was once a beginner. Your journey starts here.

Thank you for choosing Why Crypto. I am excited to have you join this revolution and to see the dreams you'll achieve along the way.

Happy reading and happy exploring!

Jithender Kumar R,
Working Professional

Acknowledgements

Writing Why Crypto has been an incredible journey, and I could not have completed this book without the support, guidance, and inspiration of many individuals. This section is my heartfelt thank-you to all those who contributed to making this dream a reality.

First and foremost, I want to express my deepest gratitude to my family, whose unwavering belief in me provided the foundation for this book. Your encouragement and patience during the countless hours I spent researching and writing have meant the world to me.

To my friends and colleagues, thank you for your valuable feedback, thought-provoking conversations, and unyielding support. Your insights helped refine the ideas and ensured this book speaks to its intended audience.

A special thanks to the cryptocurrency and blockchain communities, whose collective knowledge and openness to share have been a constant source of learning. Your passion for innovation and progress inspired much of what is written here.

To my editor and **Notionpress** publishing team, thank you for your meticulous attention to detail, thoughtful suggestions, and dedication to bringing this book to life. Your professionalism and expertise have been invaluable throughout this process.

Lastly, to you, the reader—thank you for picking up this book and embarking on this journey with me. Your curiosity and desire to learn are what make this endeavor meaningful. I hope this book serves as a useful guide and a source of inspiration as you step into the world of cryptocurrency.

This book is a collective effort, and I am deeply grateful to everyone who played a part in its creation. Thank you for being part of this journey.

With gratitude,

JK

ACKNOWLEDGEMENTS

CERTIFICATE OF PUBLISHING

We're proud to present this certificate of publishing to

Jithender Kumar

for successfully publishing

WILL I EVER BUY MY FERRARI?

on 01-04-2020

*"A writer's life and work are not a gift to mankind; **they're a necessity"*** ~ *Toni Morrison*

Image of My 1st Book - Thanks NotionPress Team for helping release my first book!

Prologue

The world is changing faster than we can sometimes comprehend. Technology has woven itself into the fabric of our daily lives, reshaping the way we communicate, work, and even think about money. Amid this whirlwind of innovation stands cryptocurrency, a digital revolution that challenges traditional financial systems and opens new doors for individuals to achieve their dreams.

For centuries, money has been at the heart of human progress—a tool that powers economies, drives ambitions, and fuels aspirations. But as the world evolves, so must our understanding of money. Cryptocurrency, born out of the desire for a decentralized and inclusive financial system, represents the next chapter in this evolution. It is not just a form of currency; it is a movement, a technology, and for many, a beacon of hope for financial freedom.

In India, a land of dreamers and innovators, the promise of cryptocurrency holds special significance. With a burgeoning population of young professionals, freelancers, and entrepreneurs, the possibilities for leveraging this technology are immense. Yet, despite its potential, crypto often feels out of reach for many—shrouded in mystery, complexity, and misinformation.

This book is my humble attempt to demystify cryptocurrency for the everyday Indian. It is a guide for those who dare to dream big but don't know where to start. It is for the curious minds who seek to understand this new frontier and for those who wish to take charge of their financial future. Through this book, I aim to simplify the concepts, provide practical insights, and inspire confidence to step into the world of crypto.

As you turn the pages, I invite you to approach this journey with an open mind and a willingness to learn. The crypto revolution is here, and it is transforming lives around the globe. Perhaps it can transform yours too.

Welcome to the future. Welcome to Why Crypto.

JK

I

Chapter 1: The Crypto Revolution

Why the World is Talking About Cryptocurrency

In recent years, cryptocurrency has become one of the most discussed topics globally, and for good reason. This digital form of currency is not controlled by any central authority, such as a government or bank, making it revolutionary. Cryptocurrencies promise financial freedom, faster transactions, and a new way to think about money.

The buzz began in 2009 when Bitcoin, the first cryptocurrency, was created by an anonymous person or group known as Satoshi Nakamoto. It was designed to solve problems inherent in traditional financial systems, such as high fees, limited accessibility, and the need for intermediaries. Since then, the crypto world has expanded, with thousands of new coins and tokens emerging to tackle various use cases.

But why is it such a hot topic? First, cryptocurrencies offer the possibility of decentralization. This means transactions occur directly between parties without relying on a middleman. Second, blockchain technology, which underpins most cryptocurrencies, provides transparency and security, ensuring all transactions are traceable and tamper-proof. Finally, crypto is a global phenomenon, enabling cross-border payments without hefty fees or delays.

As awareness grows and adoption increases, cryptocurrency is being embraced by individuals, businesses, and even governments. Major companies like Tesla, PayPal, and Microsoft now accept Bitcoin as payment, while countries like El Salvador have adopted it as legal tender. Cryptocurrencies are also gaining traction as a means to support charitable causes and fund innovative projects via crowdfunding platforms.

For Indians, this global movement represents an opportunity to participate in a digital revolution that could redefine the financial landscape. With a growing community of developers, entrepreneurs, and investors, India is uniquely positioned to leverage the benefits of cryptocurrency.

A Brief History of Money and the Rise of Crypto

To understand cryptocurrency, we must first look at the evolution of money. In ancient times, barter systems were used for trade. Over time, societies moved to commodity money, such as gold and silver, and later to coins and paper currency. In the 20th century, digital money emerged, with bank accounts and online transactions becoming the norm.

However, traditional money has limitations. It relies on central authorities, which can print more money, leading to inflation. Transactions, especially international ones, are slow and expensive due to intermediaries like banks. The 2008 global financial crisis exposed vulnerabilities in this centralized system, highlighting the need for a better alternative.

Enter Bitcoin. Created in the aftermath of the financial crisis, Bitcoin offered a decentralized, deflationary currency. Instead of being printed by governments, Bitcoin is "mined" using computational power. Its supply is capped at 21 million coins, making it resistant to inflation. As Bitcoin gained popularity, other cryptocurrencies like Ethereum, Litecoin, and Ripple were developed, each introducing unique features and use cases.

Today, the crypto ecosystem is vast, including decentralized finance (DeFi), non-fungible tokens (NFTs), and smart contracts. This evolution reflects the growing demand for innovative financial solutions and the world's shift toward digital assets.

Cryptocurrency also represents a new way of thinking about ownership and identity. Blockchain technology allows users to own their data, assets, and identities without relying on intermediaries, marking a shift toward a more equitable and transparent financial system.

Why Indians Need to Pay Attention

India is at a critical juncture when it comes to cryptocurrency. With its large population, growing tech-savvy workforce, and increasing internet penetration, India is poised to become a significant player in the crypto space. Yet, many Indians remain hesitant or unaware of the opportunities crypto offers.

For working professionals, crypto provides an avenue for passive income through investments, staking, and yield farming. Freelancers can accept payments in crypto, avoiding hefty international transaction fees. Additionally, cryptocurrencies can act as a hedge against inflation and currency devaluation, providing financial stability.

India's remittance market—one of the largest in the world—can also benefit from crypto's low-cost, fast transactions. Moreover, blockchain technology has the potential to create jobs and drive innovation in sectors like healthcare, supply chain, and governance.

While regulatory uncertainty persists, the Reserve Bank of India (RBI) and government have started exploring blockchain's potential. The recent introduction of a central bank digital currency (CBDC) further indicates the country's willingness to embrace digital assets. By understanding and adopting cryptocurrency early, Indians can position themselves to thrive in the future economy.

In addition, the Indian diaspora can leverage cryptocurrency to transfer funds back home seamlessly, saving both time and money. For young Indians, the crypto ecosystem offers opportunities to learn, innovate, and build solutions that can scale globally.

II

Chapter 2: Crypto Basics for Beginners

What is Cryptocurrency?

At its core, cryptocurrency is a digital or virtual currency that uses cryptography for security. Unlike traditional currencies issued by governments, cryptocurrencies operate on decentralized networks based on blockchain technology. This means no single entity controls them, making them transparent and resistant to censorship.

Think of cryptocurrency as a form of money that exists solely in digital form. It can be used to buy goods and services, transferred between individuals, or held as an investment. Bitcoin, the first and most well-known cryptocurrency, was designed to be a peer-to-peer electronic cash system, enabling transactions without the need for intermediaries.

Each cryptocurrency operates on its own set of rules. Some, like Bitcoin, aim to be a store of value and medium of exchange. Others, like Ethereum, focus on enabling smart contracts and decentralized applications (DApps). The key feature of cryptocurrencies is their decentralized nature, which provides users with financial sovereignty.

Cryptocurrencies also operate 24/7, unlike traditional markets that have fixed hours. This accessibility means anyone, anywhere, can participate, making it particularly attractive for people in developing countries or underbanked regions.

Understanding Blockchain Technology in Simple Terms

Blockchain is the technology that powers most cryptocurrencies. At its simplest, a blockchain is a digital ledger of transactions that is distributed across a network of computers. Each transaction is recorded in a "block," and these blocks are linked together to form a "chain."

Imagine a Google Sheet that is shared across multiple users. Anyone can view the sheet, and once a transaction is added, it cannot be altered. This ensures transparency and trust among participants. Unlike traditional databases, blockchains are decentralized, meaning no single authority controls the data. Instead, every participant in the network has a copy of the ledger.

Blockchain technology provides security through cryptography. Each block contains a unique code (called a hash) and the hash of the previous block, ensuring that any attempt to alter a transaction would be immediately detected. This makes blockchains virtually tamper-proof.

In the context of cryptocurrencies, blockchain acts as a public record of all transactions. For example, Bitcoin's blockchain records every transaction ever made with Bitcoin, ensuring transparency and accountability.

Apart from cryptocurrencies, blockchain is being used in various fields, such as supply chain management, healthcare, and real estate. Its ability to provide secure, transparent, and immutable records makes it a game-changing technology.

Types of Cryptocurrencies: Bitcoin, Ethereum, and Beyond

While Bitcoin was the first cryptocurrency and remains the most popular, the crypto world has expanded to include thousands of other coins and tokens. Here are some of the most notable ones:

1. Bitcoin (BTC): Known as the "king of crypto," Bitcoin is primarily used as a store of value and medium of exchange. Its limited supply and first-mover advantage have made it a benchmark for the entire crypto market.
2. Ethereum (ETH): Ethereum is more than a cryptocurrency; it's a platform for building decentralized applications and executing smart contracts. This makes it the backbone of decentralized finance (DeFi) and NFTs.

3. Binance Coin (BNB): Originally created to pay fees on the Binance exchange, BNB has evolved into a versatile utility token used in various applications.
4. Ripple (XRP): XRP focuses on enabling fast, low-cost international payments, making it popular among financial institutions.
5. Cardano (ADA): Known for its scientific approach, Cardano aims to create a sustainable and secure platform for DApps.
6. Solana (SOL): With its high-speed, low-cost transactions, Solana has emerged as a competitor to Ethereum in the DeFi and NFT space.
7. Polkadot (DOT): Polkadot enables different blockchains to interoperate, creating a connected ecosystem of networks.
8. Litecoin (LTC): Often referred to as the "silver to Bitcoin's gold," Litecoin is designed for faster and cheaper transactions.

Each cryptocurrency serves a unique purpose, and understanding their functions can help beginners make informed investment decisions. Whether you're looking to invest, use crypto for payments, or explore blockchain applications, the possibilities are vast and exciting.

Investors and users alike must stay informed about the rapid developments in this space, as new projects and innovations continue to emerge daily.

III

Chapter 3: Why Crypto Matters for Indians

Introduction: A Digital Revolution for a New Era

India, a land of rapid technological adoption and innovation, stands on the cusp of a digital revolution. Cryptocurrencies, with their promise of decentralization, financial inclusion, and new opportunities, are playing a pivotal role in reshaping how Indians perceive and interact with money. This chapter explores why crypto matters for Indians and how it offers unique opportunities to overcome systemic financial challenges while fostering growth and independence.

India's Growing Role in the Crypto Space

1. Adoption and Innovation

India ranks among the top countries globally in cryptocurrency adoption. From metropolitan hubs like Bengaluru and Mumbai to smaller towns, people are embracing crypto as a means to invest, trade, and build businesses. Key drivers include:

- Youth Engagement: With a median age of 28, India's young population is highly tech-savvy and open to exploring digital finance.
- Startup Ecosystem: Blockchain-based startups in India are innovating across sectors like healthcare, supply chain, and finance.
- Remittances: Crypto is revolutionizing cross-border remittances, enabling faster and cheaper transactions for millions of Indians working abroad.

Case Study: Binance, an Indian crypto exchange, saw exponential growth, highlighting the increasing demand for crypto platforms tailored to Indian users.

A map of India with hotspots highlighting cities leading in crypto adoption and innovation.

2. Government and Regulation

The Indian government's stance on cryptocurrency has been evolving. While challenges like regulatory uncertainty persist, initiatives like exploring a Central Bank Digital Currency (CBDC) demonstrate a willingness to engage with blockchain technology.

3. Global Contributions

Indian developers, entrepreneurs, and thought leaders are making significant contributions to the global crypto ecosystem. For example, Indian-origin engineers have been pivotal in developing major blockchain projects worldwide.

An infographic showing India's rising participation in global blockchain and crypto initiatives.

Financial Freedom and Opportunities for Working Professionals and Freelancers

1. Diversified Income Streams

For working professionals and freelancers, cryptocurrencies provide avenues to diversify income. From earning in crypto for global gigs to investing in decentralized finance (DeFi), possibilities are expanding.

2. Freelancing in Crypto

Platforms like Upwork and Fiverr are increasingly allowing payments in crypto, giving freelancers access to international clients without worrying about currency conversion and delays.

Case Study: Meena, a freelance graphic designer from Chennai, began accepting payments in Ethereum. This not only simplified transactions with overseas clients but also allowed her to save and grow her earnings.

3. Part-Time Traders and Investors

Busy professionals can explore part-time trading or investing. Crypto platforms often provide intuitive tools and resources for beginners, making it easy to get started with as little as INR 500.

A professional at a desk with charts showing crypto earnings alongside traditional work tasks.

4. Earning Passive Income

Crypto offers numerous passive income opportunities, such as staking, yield farming, and lending, which were covered in the previous chapter. These can complement a professional's primary income streams.

Overcoming Traditional Financial System Barriers

1. Banking Access for All

Despite progress, many Indians still lack access to traditional banking services. Cryptocurrencies bypass these barriers by enabling anyone with internet access to participate in the global economy.

Example: A small shop owner in a remote village can use a mobile crypto wallet to accept payments and access global markets.

2. Cost-Effective Remittances

India is the world's largest recipient of remittances. Traditional remittance services often involve high fees and delays. Cryptocurrencies provide a solution with lower costs and near-instant transfers.

Case Study: Rajesh, a migrant worker in Dubai, started using Bitcoin to send money home to his family in Kerala. The savings on fees allowed him to contribute more to his household.

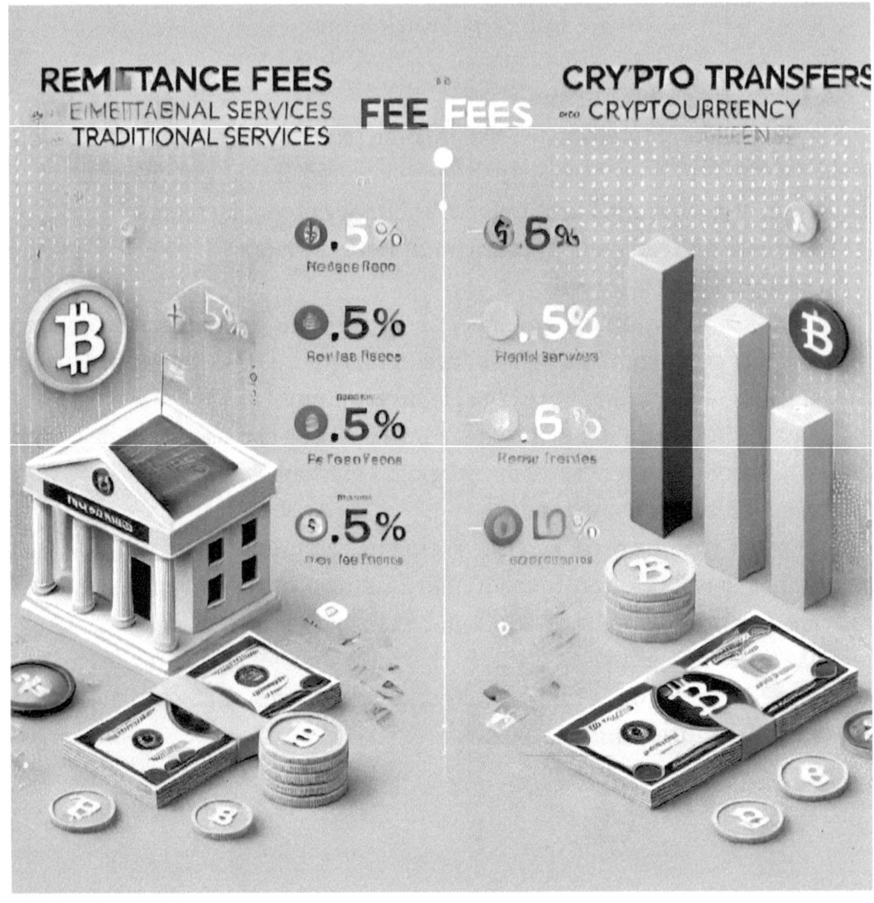

A visual comparison of remittance fees for traditional services versus crypto transfers.

3. Breaking Investment Barriers

Traditional investment avenues like real estate and stocks often require significant capital and paperwork. Cryptocurrencies offer a more accessible alternative, allowing users to invest small amounts and benefit from fractional ownership.

4. Protection Against Inflation

For many Indians, inflation erodes the value of savings. Cryptocurrencies, particularly Bitcoin, are viewed as a hedge against inflation due to their limited supply and decentralized nature.

Real-Life Stories: Crypto Empowering Indians

1. The Freelancer's Success

Sonal, a content writer from Jaipur, transitioned to accepting crypto payments from international clients. The move doubled her income and reduced dependency on traditional payment gateways.

2. Entrepreneurial Ventures

Vinod from Hyderabad launched a blockchain-based solution for supply chain management. His startup attracted global investors, showcasing how crypto can fuel entrepreneurship.

3. Breaking Financial Chains

Kavitha, a homemaker in Mumbai, started investing small amounts in crypto. Over three years, she built a substantial portfolio that gave her financial independence and a sense of empowerment.

A collage of diverse Indian individuals benefiting from crypto in different scenarios—freelancers, entrepreneurs, and homemakers.

Conclusion: A New Dawn for Indian Finance

Cryptocurrencies are not just a financial tool but a movement toward greater empowerment and inclusion. For Indians—from urban professionals to rural entrepreneurs—crypto represents an opportunity to overcome systemic barriers and achieve financial freedom. By embracing this technology, India can not only unlock individual potential but also cement its position as a global leader in the digital economy.

A sunrise over an Indian skyline with blockchain symbols subtly integrated, symbolizing a new financial dawn.

IV

Chapter 4: Decoding Crypto Investments

Introduction: Why Crypto Investments are Gaining Popularity

Investing in cryptocurrency is an exciting and revolutionary way to grow wealth. With its promise of decentralization, high returns, and innovative financial tools, crypto is attracting attention worldwide. For Indians, crypto offers new avenues for financial independence, especially for working professionals, freelancers, and those seeking passive income.

This chapter will delve into the core aspects of crypto investments, focusing on opportunities for passive income, the basics of trading, staking, and holding, and essential strategies for managing risks. By the end of this chapter, you'll have actionable insights to start or refine your crypto investment journey.

Passive Income Opportunities Through Crypto

What Makes Crypto Ideal for Passive Income?

Cryptocurrencies provide several ways to earn passive income, often with higher returns than traditional investment avenues. Unlike active trading, these methods require minimal ongoing effort after the initial setup.

Popular Passive Income Methods

1. Staking

- Definition: Locking up your cryptocurrency to support blockchain operations.

- Rewards: Earn tokens as rewards for staking.
- Example: Ramesh, an IT professional, staked INR 10,000 worth of Ethereum. Over six months, he earned a 5% return while contributing to blockchain security.

2. Yield Farming

- Definition: Providing liquidity to decentralized exchanges and earning rewards.
- Rewards: Interest or new tokens.
- Example: Meera, a freelance writer, invested in a liquidity pool on PancakeSwap. She earned a 20% annual yield on her stablecoin holdings.

3. Crypto Lending

- Definition: Lending cryptocurrency through platforms like Aave or Compound.
- Rewards: Earn interest on loans.
- Example: Anil, a small business owner, earned passive income by lending his Bitcoin holdings at an 8% annual interest rate.

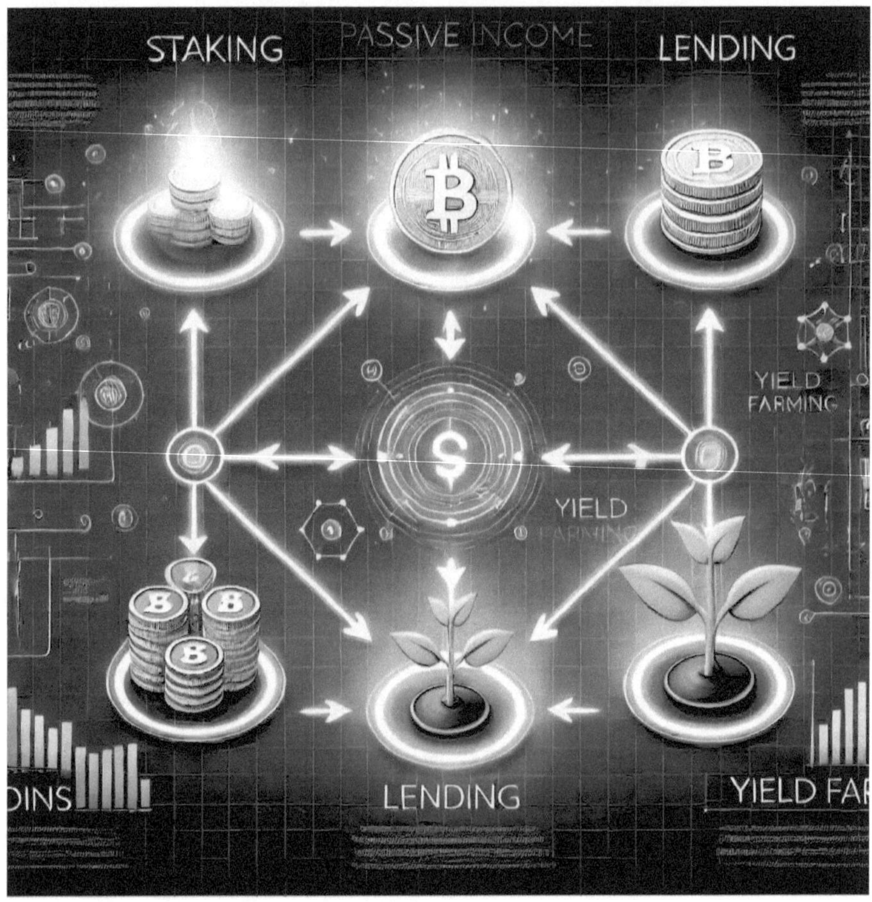

A diagram showing three streams of passive income from staking, lending, and yield farming.

Basics of Crypto Trading, Staking, and Holding

1. Crypto Trading

Trading involves buying and selling cryptocurrencies to profit from price fluctuations. Beginners should start by understanding:

- Market Basics: Learn terms like market orders, stop-loss, and limit orders.
- Platforms: Use trusted exchanges like WazirX, Binance, or Coinbase.
- Strategies: Explore day trading, swing trading, and long-term holding.

Real-Time Example: Ravi, a digital marketer, began crypto trading with INR 5,000. By analyzing market trends and setting stop-loss orders, he turned his initial investment into INR 7,000 in three months.

2. Staking

Staking allows you to earn rewards by locking your cryptocurrency in a wallet or platform to support blockchain operations. It's a low-risk option for beginners and offers predictable returns.

Steps to Start Staking:

- Select a Proof-of-Stake (PoS) cryptocurrency like Cardano or Polkadot.
- Choose a reliable staking platform or wallet.
- Lock your tokens and start earning rewards.

3. Holding (HODLing)

HODLing is the practice of holding onto your cryptocurrency for a long time, expecting its value to increase. This strategy is ideal for beginners who prefer minimal risk and activity.

Tips for Effective HODLing:

- Choose established cryptocurrencies like Bitcoin or Ethereum.
- Set a long-term goal and avoid panic selling during market dips.
- Diversify your holdings to reduce risk.

A comparison chart of trading, staking, and holding, highlighting their pros and cons.

Risk Management for Beginners

Understanding Crypto Risks

Cryptocurrency investments come with inherent risks, including:

- Volatility: Prices can fluctuate drastically within hours.
- Security Threats: Hacks and scams are common in the crypto space.
- Regulatory Uncertainty: Crypto regulations in India are still evolving.

Key Risk Management Strategies

1. Start Small

- Only invest money you can afford to lose.
- Example: Pushpa, a college professor, started with INR 2,000 in Bitcoin to test the waters without financial stress.

2. Educate Yourself

- Follow reputable crypto news platforms and forums.
- Take courses or read guides to understand market trends.

3. Diversify Your Portfolio

- Invest in multiple cryptocurrencies to mitigate risk.
- Example: Arjun diversified his holdings across Bitcoin, Ethereum, and stablecoins, reducing the impact of market fluctuations.

4. Use Secure Platforms and Wallets

- Opt for platforms with strong security features and cold storage options.
- Use hardware wallets for long-term holdings.

5. Set Clear Goals and Limits

- Decide your investment goals and stick to them.
- Example: Ritu, a freelance designer, set a goal to double her initial investment within a year and avoided impulsive trades.

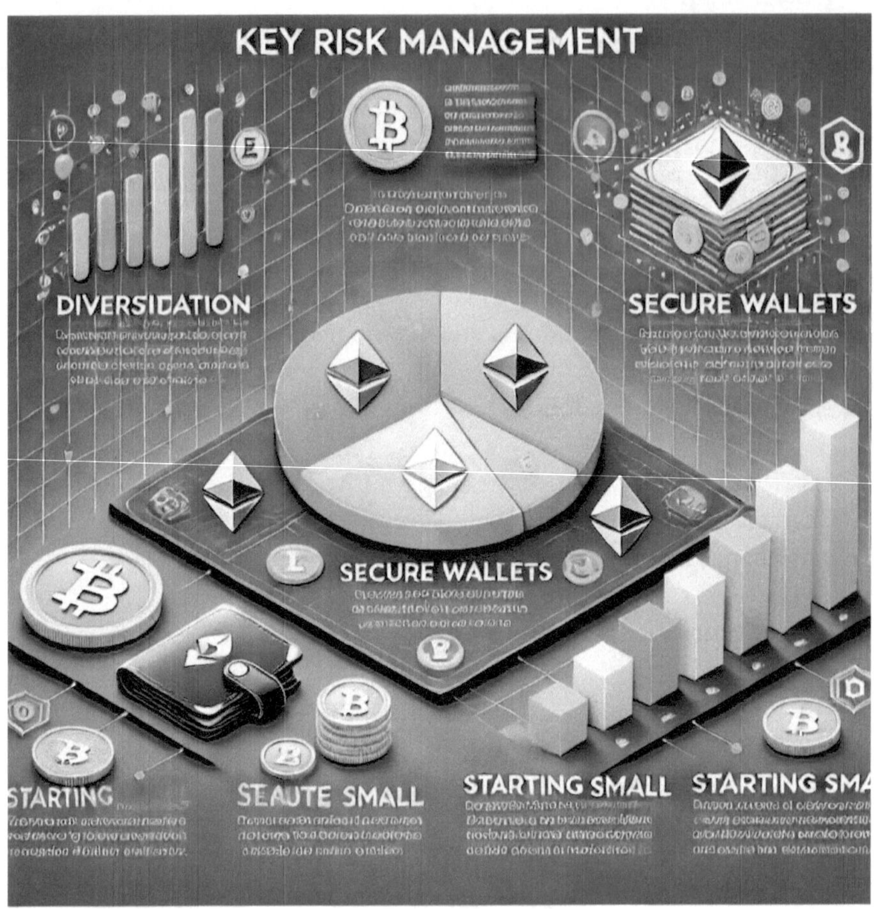

An infographic illustrating risk management strategies, including diversification, secure wallets, and starting small.

Real-Time Case Study: Combining Strategies for Success

Case Study: Vishal's Journey Vishal, a software engineer from Pune, started his crypto journey with INR 50,000. Here's how he diversified his approach:

1. Staked INR 20,000 in Cardano: Earned 5% annual returns.
2. Traded INR 10,000 in Ethereum: Made INR 2,000 profit by following market trends.

3. Holded INR 20,000 in Bitcoin: Saw a 15% increase in value over six months.

Through careful planning and risk management, Vishal grew his portfolio by 25% in one year, demonstrating the power of combining strategies.

Conclusion: Take the First Step

Crypto investments can be a game-changer for financial independence, offering diverse opportunities for passive income and growth. By understanding the basics of trading, staking, and holding, and implementing effective risk management, you can confidently navigate the crypto world. Remember, every expert was once a beginner. Start small, stay informed, and let your investments pave the way to your dreams.

A motivational image showing a roadmap labeled "Start Small," "Learn & Diversify," and "Achieve Goals" leading to a bright future.

V

Chapter 5: Getting Started with Crypto

Introduction: Taking the First Step

Venturing into the world of cryptocurrency can seem daunting, but every journey begins with a single step. For Indian working professionals, freelancers, and dreamers looking to explore this exciting space, getting started is simpler than it appears. This chapter will guide you through setting up your wallet, buying your first cryptocurrency, and safeguarding your digital assets. With practical tips and real-life stories of Indian crypto enthusiasts, you'll be ready to dive into this transformative world.

How to Set Up a Wallet

What is a Crypto Wallet?

A crypto wallet is a digital tool that allows you to store, send, and receive cryptocurrencies. Think of it as your online bank account for digital money. Wallets come in two primary forms:

1. **Hot Wallets:** Connected to the internet and easy to access, ideal for beginners. Examples include mobile apps like Trust Wallet and exchanges like Binance.
2. **Cold Wallets:** Offline wallets offering higher security, such as hardware wallets like Ledger Nano or Trezor.

Steps to Set Up a Wallet

1. **Choose the Right Wallet:** Decide between a hot or cold wallet based on your needs.
2. **Download and Install:** Visit the official website or app store to download your wallet.
3. **Create an Account:** Follow the prompts to set up your account. You'll need to create a strong password.
4. **Save Your Seed Phrase:** Your wallet will generate a recovery seed phrase. Write this down and keep it secure.

Real Story: Arjun's Journey with His First Wallet

Arjun, a tech-savvy marketing professional from Mumbai, started his crypto journey with a Trust Wallet. After following tutorials and securing his seed phrase, he began exploring Bitcoin and Ethereum. He recalls, "I felt empowered to control my own money without relying on banks."

A step-by-step graphic on setting up a crypto wallet, showing key steps like downloading, creating an account, and saving the seed phrase.

Buying Your First Cryptocurrency: Exchanges and Platforms

Choosing the Right Exchange

Cryptocurrency exchanges are platforms where you can buy, sell, or trade cryptocurrencies. Popular options for Indians include:

- **Binance:** A global exchange with a vast selection of cryptocurrencies.
- **CoinDCX:** Known for its intuitive interface and security features.

Step-by-Step Guide to Buying Crypto

1. **Sign Up on an Exchange:** Register with your email and phone number.
2. **Complete KYC:** Submit identity documents like Aadhaar or PAN for verification.
3. **Deposit Funds:** Transfer INR using UPI, net banking, or other payment methods.
4. **Choose a Cryptocurrency:** Start with popular options like Bitcoin or Ethereum.
5. **Make Your First Purchase:** Enter the amount and confirm the transaction.

Real Story: Sneha's First Bitcoin Purchase

Sneha, a freelance graphic designer from Pune, bought her first Bitcoin on Binance with just 1,000 INR. She shares, "The process was simpler than I imagined. I started small and learned as I went."

A screenshot of a crypto exchange interface, highlighting the process of selecting a cryptocurrency and making a purchase.

Security Essentials: Avoiding Scams and Safeguarding Assets
Common Crypto Scams

1. **Phishing Attacks:** Fake websites or emails that steal login credentials.
2. **Ponzi Schemes:** Fraudulent schemes promising high returns.
3. **Fake Wallets and Apps:** Malicious apps designed to steal your funds.

How to Stay Safe

1. **Use Trusted Platforms:** Stick to well-known exchanges and wallets.
2. **Enable Two-Factor Authentication (2FA):** Adds an extra layer of security.
3. **Beware of Scams:** Avoid offers that sound too good to be true.
4. **Store Assets Securely:** Use cold wallets for long-term storage.

Real Story: Rajesh's Experience with a Scam

Ashwin, a software developer from Bengaluru, fell victim to a phishing attack. "I clicked on a fake link and lost access to my wallet," he recounts. He now uses a hardware wallet and ensures all links are verified before clicking.

A visual warning sign illustrating common crypto scams, such as phishing emails and fake platforms.

Practical Tips for Beginners

1. **Start Small:** Begin with an amount you can afford to lose.
2. **Educate Yourself:** Follow trusted sources and stay updated on crypto trends.
3. **Diversify Your Portfolio:** Don't put all your funds into one cryptocurrency.
4. **Test Transactions:** Practice with small amounts to understand how transfers work.

Conclusion: Taking Charge of Your Financial Future

Getting started with crypto is an empowering experience. By setting up a wallet, making your first purchase, and prioritizing security, you're taking control of your financial future. Remember, every expert was once a beginner. With the right steps and caution, your journey into cryptocurrency can be both rewarding and secure.

A motivational image of an Indian family discussing financial goals with a laptop displaying a crypto wallet.

VI

Chapter 6: Making Crypto Work for You

Introduction: A New Financial Frontier

Cryptocurrency is more than an investment vehicle; it's a tool that can empower you to reshape your financial future. For Indians navigating the gig economy, looking to build wealth, or planning for long-term goals, crypto offers opportunities that are both accessible and transformative. In this chapter, we'll explore how to earn crypto, diversify your holdings, and implement growth strategies for lasting financial success. Real stories of Indians who have embraced crypto will illustrate the practical applications of these strategies.

Earning Crypto: Freelancing and Crypto Payments

Freelancing in the Crypto Era

Freelancers in India—whether graphic designers, content writers, or software developers—have discovered that accepting crypto payments can open doors to global clients and higher earnings.

1. Why Accept Crypto?

- Faster payments: Bypass traditional banking delays.
- Lower fees: Reduce costs associated with currency conversions and wire transfers.
- Global reach: Access international clients without financial barriers.

2. Platforms Supporting Crypto Payments

- Upwork and Fiverr: Some clients offer crypto as a payment option.
- Crypto-Specific Platforms: Sites like Cryptogrind or LaborX cater exclusively to freelancers looking for crypto payments.

3. How to Get Started

- Create a crypto wallet to receive payments.
- Update your freelancing profiles to mention your acceptance of crypto.
- Educate yourself about taxation to stay compliant with Indian laws.

Real Story: Priya's Freelancing Journey

Priya, a digital marketer from Hyderabad, started accepting payments in Bitcoin for her services. With crypto payments, she eliminated international transaction fees and reinvested her earnings in Ethereum. Over two years, her crypto portfolio grew by 50%, helping her fund a long-awaited family vacation to Europe.

Illustration of a freelancer's workflow with payments flowing into a digital wallet.

Building a Diversified Portfolio

Why Diversify?

A diversified portfolio minimizes risks and maximizes returns by spreading investments across various assets. In the crypto world, this means balancing established coins like Bitcoin and Ethereum with promising altcoins and stablecoins.

1. Key Components of a Crypto Portfolio

- Bitcoin and Ethereum: Reliable and dominant assets for stability.

- Altcoins: Tokens like Cardano, Solana, or Polkadot with growth potential.
- Stablecoins: Assets like USDT or USDC to mitigate volatility.

2. Strategies for Diversification

- Percentage Allocation: Dedicate 60% to Bitcoin/Ethereum, 30% to altcoins, and 10% to stablecoins.
- Sector Diversification: Invest in coins related to DeFi, gaming, and infrastructure.
- Regular Rebalancing: Adjust allocations periodically to align with market trends.

3. Tools for Portfolio Management

- Apps like CoinStats and Delta for tracking performance.
- Exchanges offering portfolio insights, such as Binance and WazirX.

Real Story: Arjun's Balanced Approach

Sakshi, a software engineer in Bengaluru, started investing INR 5,000 monthly in Bitcoin. Later, he added altcoins like Polygon and Aave, drawn to their technological potential. By diversifying, he balanced high-risk, high-reward investments with more stable returns, growing his wealth steadily over five years.

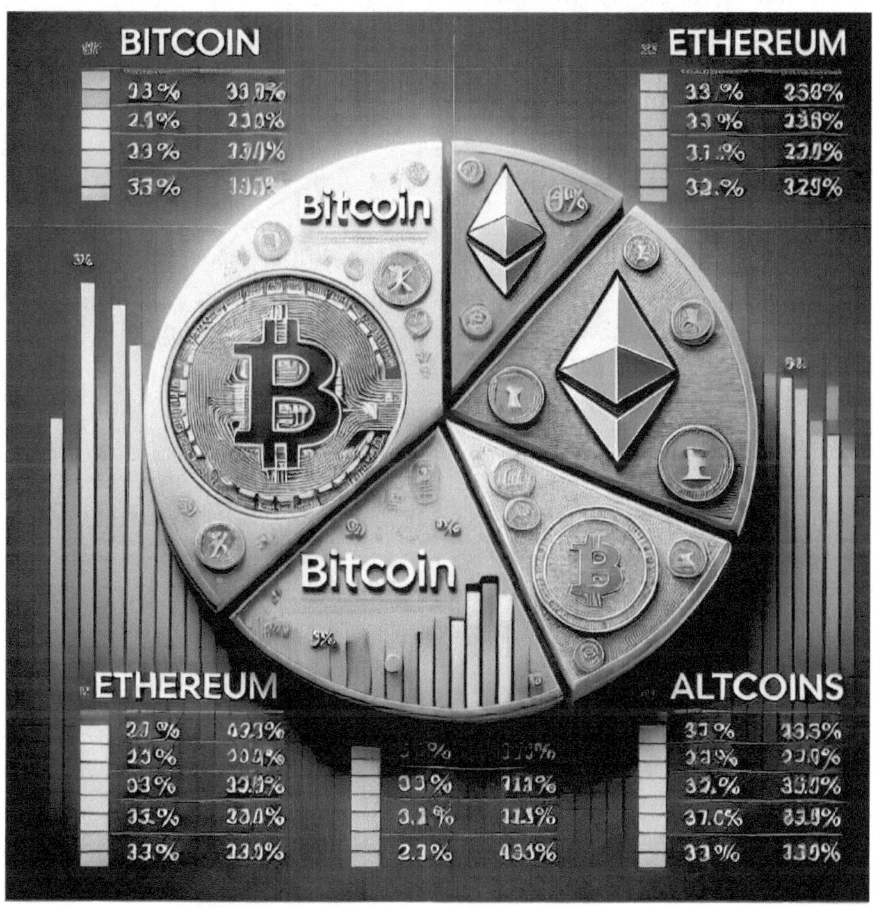

A pie chart of a diversified crypto portfolio with percentages allocated to Bitcoin, Ethereum, and altcoins.

Long-Term Growth Strategies

The Importance of Patience

Crypto's volatility can be intimidating, but adopting a long-term perspective often yields significant rewards. Indian investors who held Bitcoin or Ethereum for five or more years have seen exponential growth.

1. HODLing (Holding On for Dear Life)

- Resist the urge to sell during market downturns.
- Invest only what you can afford to lock away for years.

2. Staking for Passive Income

- Stake coins like Ethereum or Solana to earn rewards while holding.
- Use platforms like Binance or Coinbase to simplify the process.

3. Cost Averaging

- Invest a fixed amount regularly (e.g., INR 1,000 per week) to mitigate volatility.
- Platforms like CoinSwitch Kuber make systematic investment easy.

4. Stay Informed

- Follow industry news and updates to identify long-term opportunities.
- Join Indian crypto communities on Telegram or Twitter to share insights.

Real Story: Misheal's Path to Financial Freedom

Misheal, a teacher in Pune, started investing in Bitcoin in 2016 with just INR 1,000 monthly. Despite market dips, she remained patient, learning about staking and cost averaging. By 2023, her portfolio's value exceeded INR 50 lakhs, enabling her to retire early and start a passion project.

A timeline showing the growth of Neha's portfolio over the years, with milestones marked.

Common Pitfalls to Avoid

1. Over-Investing in a Single Asset

- Diversify to protect against market-specific crashes.

2. Reacting to FOMO

- Avoid impulsive decisions driven by hype.

3. Ignoring Security

- Use two-factor authentication and cold wallets to secure your assets.

Conclusion: Turning Knowledge into Action

Earning, investing, and growing through crypto requires knowledge, discipline, and a willingness to adapt. By learning from real-life experiences and following proven strategies, you can make crypto work for you, helping you achieve your dreams and financial independence.

An inspiring image of an Indian family using a laptop, with a glowing Bitcoin symbol in the background, symbolizing a future built on crypto.

VII

Chapter 7: Crypto as a Tool to Achieve Dreams

Introduction: Turning Dreams into Reality with Crypto

Cryptocurrency is more than just a digital asset; for many, it has become a tool to transform their lives. From achieving financial independence to funding passions, crypto has enabled countless individuals to reach goals they once thought impossible. For Indians, where financial constraints and limited opportunities often hinder dreams, crypto offers a new horizon of possibilities.

In this chapter, we will explore inspiring stories of Indians who leveraged crypto to build their dreams, understand how crypto can enable financial independence, and learn to set achievable goals using cryptocurrency investments. By the end of this chapter, you'll be equipped with the motivation and knowledge to begin your journey toward using crypto as a tool to achieve your own dreams.

Stories of People Who Used Crypto to Build Their Dreams

1. Ravi's Journey to Entrepreneurial Success

Ravi, a 32-year-old software engineer from Pune, always dreamed of starting his own tech company but lacked the capital. In 2017, he began investing in Bitcoin and Ethereum with small amounts from his salary. Over time, his investments grew significantly. By 2021, he had amassed enough wealth to quit his job and launch his own AI startup.

> “*"Crypto gave me the financial boost I needed to chase my dreams," says Ravi. "It wasn't just about the money—it was about believing in a vision."*”

A young Indian entrepreneur working on a laptop, with a Bitcoin logo subtly displayed in the background.

2. Meera's Journey to Financial Independence

Meera, a single mother from Jaipur, struggled to make ends meet with her job as a school teacher. In 2020, she started staking Cardano after learning about it through a friend. The passive income she earned allowed her to pay off debts and save for her daughter's education.

"Crypto empowered me to provide a better future for my child," says Meera. "I never thought I could achieve this level of financial independence."

An Indian mother and daughter sitting together with books and a laptop showing a crypto wallet on the screen.

3. Arjun's Global Travel Dream

Arjun, a travel enthusiast from Bengaluru, wanted to explore the world but couldn't afford the expenses. In 2018, he began yield farming on DeFi platforms and reinvested his earnings. By 2022, he had saved enough to fund a year-long trip across Europe and Southeast Asia.

> *"Crypto opened the door to experiences I only dreamed about," shares Arjun. "It's about using the opportunities wisely."*

An Indian traveler with a backpack, standing in front of a global landmark like the Eiffel Tower, with crypto symbols in the background.

From Passive Income to Financial Independence

The Power of Passive Income

Passive income is the foundation of financial independence, and crypto provides multiple ways to achieve it:

1. **Staking:** Earn rewards by holding cryptocurrencies like Ethereum or Solana.
2. **Lending:** Provide crypto loans and earn interest through platforms like Aave.
3. **Yield Farming:** Generate returns by providing liquidity to decentralized exchanges.

Real-Life Impact

Passive income through crypto enables:

- Paying off loans or mortgages.
- Saving for children's education.
- Pursuing personal passions or starting a business.

Case Study: Sneha's Path to Independence

Sneha, a freelance graphic designer from Delhi, used yield farming to supplement her irregular income. By 2022, she earned enough to buy her own apartment in Gurgaon, fulfilling her long-cherished dream.

A modern Indian woman standing proudly in front of her new home, holding a tablet displaying crypto earnings.

Setting Realistic Goals with Crypto Investments

Why Setting Goals Matters

Investing in crypto without a clear purpose can lead to losses and missed opportunities. Setting realistic goals helps align your investments with your aspirations.

Steps to Goal Setting

1. **Define Your Dream:** Whether it's buying a house, funding education, or starting a business, be specific.

2. **Determine the Financial Requirement:** Calculate the amount needed to achieve your goal.
3. **Choose the Right Investment Strategy:** Align your goals with suitable crypto strategies like long-term holding or staking.
4. **Set a Timeline:** Establish a realistic timeline to achieve your objective.

Example: Rohit's Investment Plan

Rohit, a young IT professional from Hyderabad, aimed to save 10 lakhs INR for his wedding in three years. He invested in Bitcoin and Ethereum, reinvested his staking rewards, and reached his target six months early.

> *"Crypto taught me discipline and patience," says Rohit. "It's not just an investment; it's a journey."*

An Indian couple celebrating an engagement, with subtle crypto elements like a Bitcoin cake topper or crypto-themed decorations.

Action Item: Start Your Crypto Journey Today
To make crypto a tool for achieving your dreams:

1. Identify a specific goal you want to achieve.
2. Research and choose a crypto strategy aligned with that goal.
3. Start with a small, manageable investment to build confidence.
4. Monitor your progress and adjust your approach as needed.

Remember, the journey of a thousand miles begins with a single step. Let crypto be the bridge to your dreams!

A motivational graphic showing an Indian family or individual looking at a "roadmap to dreams" with milestones marked as crypto investments.

By reading this chapter, you've seen how ordinary Indians turned their dreams into reality through crypto. Your dreams are within reach, too—take the first step today and embrace the possibilities.

VIII

Chapter 8: Challenges and Myths About Crypto

Introduction: Separating Fact from Fiction

Cryptocurrency is one of the most talked-about topics in the financial world today, but it's also surrounded by myths, misconceptions, and challenges. For Indians who are new to crypto, these myths can create unnecessary fear, while the challenges might seem insurmountable. This chapter will tackle the common misconceptions, explain the regulatory landscape in India, and provide strategies to handle market volatility.

By the end of this chapter, you'll have a clearer understanding of what's true, what's not, and how to navigate the challenges of crypto responsibly.

Common Misconceptions and Truths

Misconception 1: Cryptocurrency is Only for Criminals

- **The Myth:** Many believe that crypto is primarily used for illegal activities like money laundering and drug trafficking.
- **The Truth:** While crypto has been used for such purposes, studies show that illicit transactions make up less than 1% of crypto activity. Blockchain's transparency actually makes it easier to track and trace transactions compared to cash.

Misconception 2: Cryptocurrency is a Get-Rich-Quick Scheme

- The Myth: Some view crypto as a magical way to make money overnight.

- The Truth: While early adopters have made significant gains, crypto investment requires research, patience, and risk management. It's not a guaranteed way to become wealthy.

Misconception 3: Cryptocurrency is Not Secure

- **The Myth:** People think that crypto wallets and exchanges are easily hacked.
- **The Truth:** Security depends on how you manage your crypto. Using secure wallets, enabling two-factor authentication, and avoiding scams can significantly reduce risks.

Misconception 4: Cryptocurrency Has No Real-World Use

- **The Myth:** Critics argue that crypto has no practical applications.
- **The Truth:** From remittances and smart contracts to decentralized finance (DeFi) and gaming, crypto is being used across industries to solve real-world problems.

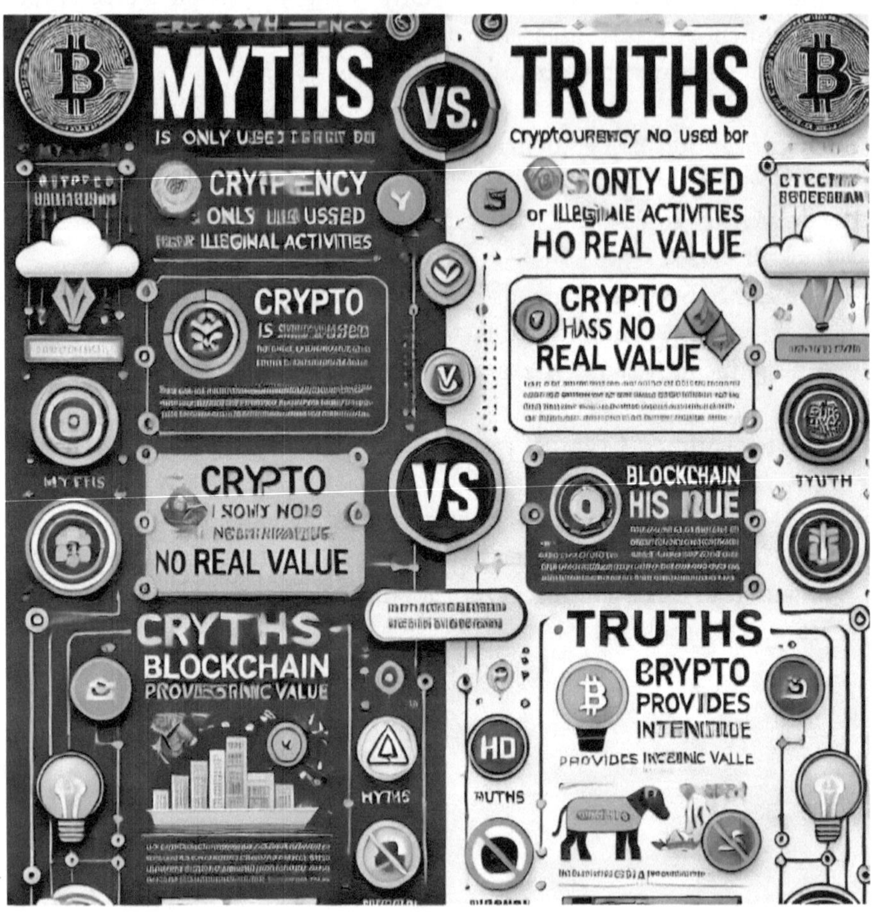

A debunking infographic showing myths versus truths about cryptocurrency.

Crypto Regulations in India

The Current Regulatory Landscape

India's stance on cryptocurrency has evolved over the years. While the government has not banned crypto, it has introduced taxation and compliance measures. Here's an overview:

1. **Taxation:** As of 2022, a 30% tax is levied on crypto gains, and a 1% TDS applies to transactions.

2. **Legal Status:** Cryptocurrencies are not yet classified as legal tender in India.
3. **RBI's CBDC:** The Reserve Bank of India (RBI) is working on its own Central Bank Digital Currency (CBDC), which will coexist with private cryptocurrencies.
4. **KYC and AML Requirements:** Exchanges must comply with Know Your Customer (KYC) and Anti-Money Laundering (AML) norms.

What to Expect in the Future

- **Regulatory Clarity:** As crypto adoption grows, the government is likely to introduce clearer guidelines.
- **Institutional Involvement:** More traditional financial institutions may embrace crypto.
- **Global Collaboration:** India might align its regulations with global standards to attract investment.

Staying Compliant

- Use registered exchanges that follow Indian regulations.
- Keep records of all transactions for tax purposes.
- Stay updated on government announcements.

Trending Question: Will India ban cryptocurrencies?

Answer: While there has been speculation, the government's actions so far indicate a focus on regulation rather than an outright ban. It's more likely that India will establish a framework to govern the use and trade of crypto responsibly.

A timeline of India's crypto regulatory developments.

Handling Volatility and Staying Informed
Understanding Crypto Volatility

Cryptocurrencies are known for their price swings. Here's why:

1. **Market Sentiment:** News, tweets, and market speculation can drive sudden changes.
2. **Liquidity:** Smaller market size compared to traditional assets makes crypto more sensitive to trades.
3. **Lack of Regulation:** Absence of centralized oversight can lead to price manipulation.

Strategies to Manage Volatility

1. **Start Small:** Invest only what you can afford to lose.
2. **Diversify:** Don't put all your money into one cryptocurrency.
3. **Use Stop-Loss Orders:** Protect your investments from significant downturns.
4. **Stay Long-Term:** Focus on long-term growth instead of short-term fluctuations.

Staying Informed

1. **Follow Reliable Sources:** Subscribe to credible news platforms like CoinDesk and CryptoSlate.
2. **Join Communities:** Participate in forums, Telegram groups, and Twitter discussions.
3. **Learn Continuously:** Take online courses or attend webinars on blockchain and crypto.
4. **Beware of Misinformation:** Verify claims before making decisions.

Trending Question: How can I predict the crypto market?

- **Answer:** Predicting the crypto market is nearly impossible due to its complexity. Instead, focus on understanding trends, staying updated, and diversifying your investments.

A candlestick chart showing crypto price fluctuations, with annotations explaining key movements.

Case Studies: Overcoming Challenges

1. **Amit's Journey:** How a freelancer navigated crypto taxation in India and still grew his portfolio.
2. **Rina's Lesson:** A working professional who lost money due to FOMO but recovered by adopting a disciplined investment strategy.
3. **Vikram's Approach:** A passive income seeker who used staking to earn steady returns while avoiding high-risk investments.

Conclusion: Empowering Yourself with Knowledge

Crypto's challenges can be daunting, but they're not insurmountable. By debunking myths, understanding regulations, and learning to manage volatility, you can approach crypto with confidence. Remember, knowledge is your best tool for overcoming obstacles in this exciting and evolving space.

A motivational image showing a person breaking through barriers labeled "Myths" and "Challenges" toward a brighter future marked "Opportunities.

IX

Chapter 9: The Future of Crypto in India

Introduction: A Glimpse into the Future

The cryptocurrency revolution is at a critical juncture, especially in India. With over 1.4 billion people, a rapidly growing digital economy, and an increasing interest in financial independence, the potential for crypto adoption in India is enormous. In this chapter, we will explore emerging trends in the crypto world, the evolving stance of the Indian government, and the transformative opportunities offered by decentralized finance (DeFi).

Emerging Trends in the Crypto World

The global cryptocurrency market is evolving at breakneck speed. India, as a tech-savvy nation, is uniquely positioned to benefit from these trends. Let's delve into some key developments shaping the future:

1. Mainstream Adoption of Crypto

- Global brands like Tesla, Microsoft, and PayPal are integrating crypto payments.
- In India, fintech platforms such as WazirX and CoinSwitch Kuber are making crypto accessible to millions.
- A recent survey by Chainalysis (2023) ranked India among the top five countries for crypto adoption.

2. The Rise of Stablecoins

- Stablecoins like USDT and USDC provide a bridge between volatile crypto markets and traditional fiat currencies.
- In India, freelancers and export businesses increasingly use stablecoins to receive payments, bypassing high transaction fees.

3. NFTs and the Creator Economy

- Non-fungible tokens (NFTs) are enabling Indian artists, musicians, and creators to monetize their work directly.
- Bollywood celebrities like Amitabh Bachchan and Salman Khan have launched their own NFT collections.

4. Green Cryptocurrencies

- With concerns about Bitcoin's energy consumption, eco-friendly cryptos like Chia and Cardano are gaining traction.
- India's focus on renewable energy aligns well with this trend.

A visual showcasing trends like stablecoins, NFTs, and green cryptos with icons and short descriptions.

How the Indian Government is Shaping the Crypto Landscape

The Indian government's stance on cryptocurrency has been dynamic, oscillating between caution and innovation. Understanding the regulatory framework is key to navigating the future of crypto in India.

1. The Crypto Tax Regime

- In 2022, the government introduced a 30% tax on crypto gains and a 1% TDS on transactions.
- While this created challenges, it also legitimized crypto as a taxable asset.

- Latest data (2023) from the Ministry of Finance indicates over ₹1,500 crore collected in crypto taxes, highlighting growing participation.

2. Regulatory Sandboxes

- The Reserve Bank of India (RBI) has launched sandboxes to test blockchain applications in financial services.
- These initiatives aim to foster innovation while ensuring consumer protection.

3. The Digital Rupee Initiative

- The RBI's Central Bank Digital Currency (CBDC) pilot is set to revolutionize payments by providing a government-backed digital currency.
- As of late 2023, over 500,000 merchants across India are part of the Digital Rupee trial.

4. Global Collaborations

- India is engaging with G20 nations to establish a unified global framework for crypto regulation.
- This initiative could position India as a leader in shaping global crypto policies.

Challenges Ahead

- **Lack of Clarity:** Ambiguity in laws discourages institutional investors.
- **Security Concerns:** Ensuring the safety of crypto platforms and user assets is paramount.

A timeline showing key government actions like the 2022 tax regime, CBDC pilot, and G20 discussions.

Opportunities in Decentralized Finance (DeFi)

Decentralized finance is transforming how people interact with financial systems, eliminating intermediaries and offering innovative solutions. For India, with its vast unbanked population, DeFi could be a game-changer.

1. What is DeFi?

DeFi refers to financial services built on blockchain technology that operate without centralized institutions. Key services include:

- Lending and borrowing platforms (e.g., Aave, Compound)

- Decentralized exchanges (e.g., Uniswap, PancakeSwap)
- Stablecoin-based savings accounts

2. How DeFi Can Empower Indians

- **Financial Inclusion:** Over 190 million Indians remain unbanked. DeFi platforms can provide access to loans, savings, and investments without the need for traditional banks.
- **Lower Costs:** By cutting out intermediaries, DeFi reduces transaction fees, making financial services more affordable.
- **Global Access:** DeFi platforms are borderless, enabling Indians to invest in global markets without restrictions.

3. DeFi Innovations Relevant to India

- **Microloans:** Platforms like Goldfinch are providing small-scale loans to entrepreneurs in developing countries, including India.
- **Tokenized Assets:** Real estate and commodities are being tokenized, making them more accessible to retail investors.
- **Smart Contracts:** Automated agreements ensure transparency and reduce fraud.

4. The Risks of DeFi

- **Smart Contract Vulnerabilities:** Bugs in code can lead to significant losses.
- **Regulatory Uncertainty:** The lack of oversight makes DeFi both an opportunity and a risk.
- **Market Volatility:** DeFi tokens can be highly unpredictable.

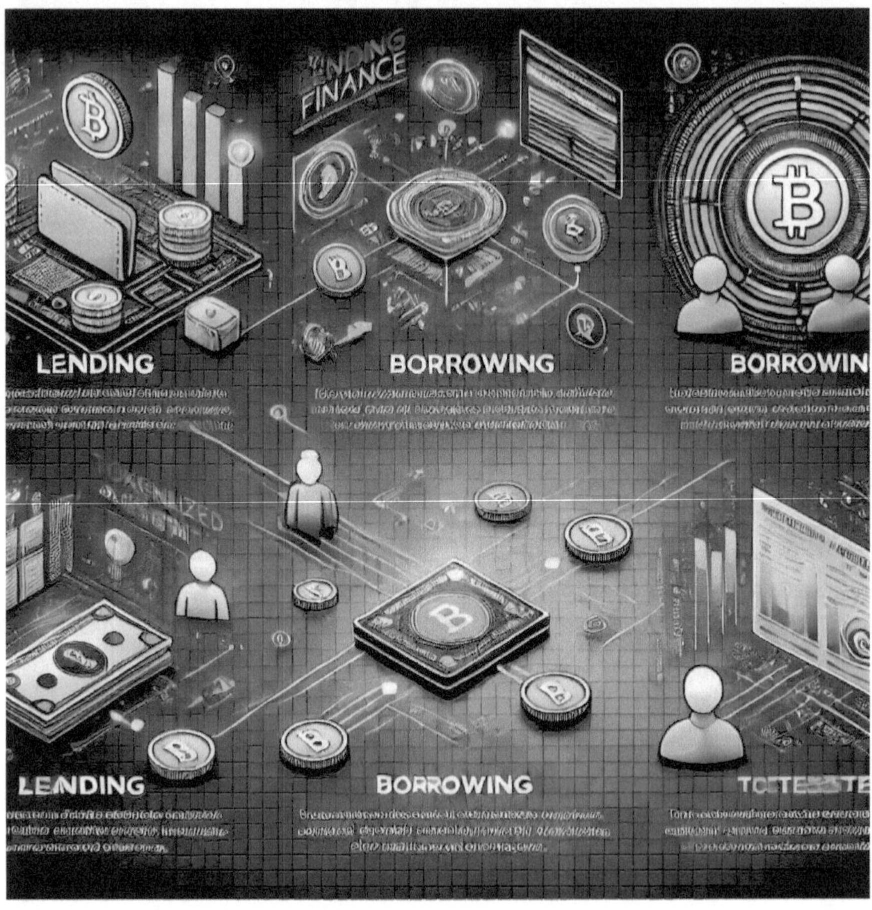

An infographic showing DeFi applications like lending, borrowing, and tokenized assets, with visual examples.

Case Studies: Real-Life Impact of Crypto in India

- **Crypto for Freelancers:** Ramesh, a freelance developer from Hyderabad, uses stablecoins to receive international payments instantly, saving on conversion fees.
- **DeFi for Farmers:** A pilot project in Maharashtra leveraged DeFi to provide microloans to farmers, reducing reliance on traditional moneylenders.

- **NFTs for Artists:** Meera, a digital artist from Delhi, sold her artwork as NFTs, earning ₹10 lakh in a global marketplace.

A collage of freelancers, farmers, and artists benefiting from crypto.

Conclusion: India's Role in the Global Crypto Ecosystem

India's journey with cryptocurrency is just beginning. The country has the talent, ambition, and market potential to become a global leader in this space. By embracing emerging trends, navigating regulatory challenges, and leveraging opportunities in DeFi, Indians can unlock the full potential of the crypto revolution.

The future is bright, but it requires collaboration between individuals, businesses, and the government to build a robust and inclusive crypto ecosystem. As you finish this chapter, remember that your journey into crypto can contribute to shaping India's digital future.

A vision of India's crypto future with iconic landmarks like the Gateway of India and blockchain elements integrated into the skyline.

X

Chapter 10: Your Crypto Journey Starts Here

Introduction: The Beginning of an Exciting Journey

The decision to embark on a crypto journey is a significant step toward financial empowerment and achieving your dreams. Cryptocurrency, once seen as a niche investment, is now a global phenomenon transforming industries and individual lives. This chapter is your gateway to starting with crypto the right way, building the mindset necessary for success, and leveraging opportunities like the Beldex Coin community to accelerate your journey.

Step-by-Step Guide to Start Today

Starting with cryptocurrency can feel overwhelming, but breaking it down into manageable steps makes it achievable:

1. Understand the Basics

Before diving in, educate yourself about cryptocurrency, blockchain, and key terms like wallets, exchanges, and tokens. Books, trusted websites, and beginner-friendly courses are excellent resources.

2. Choose a Reliable Exchange and Wallet

Select a secure platform for buying and trading cryptocurrency. Use a hardware or software wallet to store your assets securely.

3. Start Small

Invest an amount you can afford to lose while you learn. Start with popular and stable cryptocurrencies like Bitcoin or Ethereum before exploring others like Beldex Coin.

4. Practice with Simulators

Several platforms offer virtual trading environments where you can practice investing without risking real money.

5. Join Crypto Communities

Connect with like-minded individuals in forums, Telegram groups, or local meetups. Learning from others can provide valuable insights.

6. Stay Informed

Follow crypto news, updates, and regulations to make informed decisions. Knowledge is your most powerful tool in this volatile space.

![Image Suggestion: A simple roadmap illustration showing steps from learning to investing in crypto.]

Building the Right Mindset for Success

Cryptocurrency is not just about technology or finance—it's also about mindset. Here's how to develop a winning approach:

1. Patience is Key

Crypto investments often require long-term vision. Markets are volatile, and significant gains usually come to those who wait.

2. Embrace Risk with Caution

Understand that volatility is part of the game. Diversify your portfolio to balance risks and rewards.

3. Learn from Failures

Even seasoned investors face setbacks. Treat mistakes as opportunities to learn and grow.

4. Stay Disciplined

Stick to your investment plan and avoid emotional decisions driven by fear or greed.

5. Adapt to Changes

Crypto evolves rapidly. Stay curious, adaptable, and open to learning about new trends and opportunities.

A motivational image showing a person climbing stairs labeled "Patience," "Discipline," and "Adaptability" leading to a success flag.

Achieving Your Dreams, One Coin at a Time

Crypto is more than just an investment—it's a tool to achieve financial independence and personal goals. Here's how to align your crypto journey with your dreams:

1. Define Your Goals

Be clear about why you're investing in crypto. Whether it's buying a home, funding education, or retiring early, having a goal keeps you focused.

2. Automate Your Investments

Set up systematic investment plans (SIPs) to regularly invest in crypto, leveraging cost averaging to reduce risk.

3. Reinvest Gains

Use earnings from staking, yield farming, or trading to compound your wealth.

4. Celebrate Milestones

Acknowledge small achievements on your journey. This keeps you motivated and reinforces positive habits.

Case Study: Radhika, a teacher from Delhi, used systematic investments in crypto to save for her daughter's education. By investing INR 5,000 monthly over three years, she saw her portfolio grow by 150%, enabling her to achieve her goal.

A vision board illustration featuring dreams like a house, education, and travel with crypto coins symbolizing pathways.

Beldex Coin: A Gateway to Community and Growth

Introduction to Beldex Coin

Beldex Coin is a promising cryptocurrency that combines privacy and utility. Built on innovative blockchain technology, it focuses on secure, private, and decentralized transactions, making it a unique addition to the crypto ecosystem.

Why Beldex Coin Stands Out

- **Privacy-Focused:** Protects user data with advanced encryption.
- **Scalability:** Efficient and fast transactions.
- **Community-Driven:** Backed by a growing global and Indian community.

The Promising Future of Beldex Coin

1. **Integration in Real-World Applications** Beldex Coin is expanding its use cases in payment systems, decentralized finance (DeFi), and beyond.
2. **Strong Development Team** With continuous upgrades and innovations, Beldex ensures it stays ahead in the crypto space.
3. **Supportive Ecosystem** By joining the Beldex community, you'll access resources, support, and opportunities for trading and staking Beldex Coins.

Joining the Beldex Business Community

Becoming part of the Beldex family offers several benefits:

- **Education and Training:** Learn the intricacies of crypto and blockchain.
- **Networking Opportunities:** Connect with professionals and enthusiasts.
- **Trading Support:** Access tools and platforms tailored for Beldex Coin trading.

Case Study: Jamil, a business owner in Pondicherry, joined the Beldex community to diversify his income streams. With guidance and support from AARMAN community & Titan Leaders, he successfully integrated Beldex Coin into his financial strategy, enhancing both privacy and profitability.

A welcoming image showing a group of diverse individuals with a banner reading"Welcome to the Beldex Family."

Conclusion: Your Journey Begins Now

Your decision to explore cryptocurrency is a bold and exciting step toward financial independence and achieving your dreams. With the right mindset, strategies, and support from communities like Beldex, the possibilities are endless. Remember, every great journey begins with a single step. Start today, stay committed, and watch as your dreams unfold, one coin at a time.

An inspirational image of a sunrise with the text "Your Crypto Journey Starts Here."

XI

Chapter 11: Importance of KYC in the Cryptocurrency World

Introduction: Understanding KYC in Cryptocurrency

Know Your Customer (KYC) is a critical process in the financial and cryptocurrency sectors. It refers to the practices employed by institutions to verify the identity of their clients. As the crypto market grows, KYC has become an essential step for exchanges, wallet providers, and financial institutions to prevent illegal activities such as money laundering, fraud, and terrorism financing.

For Indian users, the implementation of KYC in crypto platforms plays a pivotal role in building trust and ensuring compliance with government regulations. This chapter explores the importance of KYC in the crypto world, its benefits, and how to complete the process step by step.

Why KYC is Crucial in Cryptocurrency

1. Prevention of Financial Crimes

KYC helps to identify and track individuals involved in illicit activities. By verifying users' identities, crypto platforms can flag suspicious transactions and prevent money laundering.

2. Enhancing Trust and Credibility

Platforms that implement robust KYC procedures build trust among their users. For Indian investors, this trust is crucial in adopting cryptocurrencies as a legitimate asset class.

3. Compliance with Regulations

The Reserve Bank of India (RBI) and other global regulators emphasize the importance of KYC to maintain financial integrity. By adhering to KYC norms, crypto platforms can avoid legal complications and ensure smooth operations.

4. Protecting User Funds

KYC reduces the risk of fraud and scams by ensuring that only verified users can access crypto services. This added layer of security safeguards user funds and data.

Infographic showing the role of KYC in preventing fraud, enhancing trust, and ensuring compliance.

The KYC Process: Step-by-Step Guide
Step 1: Registration

- Visit the official website or app of the crypto exchange or platform you want to use.
- Create an account by providing basic details such as email address, phone number, and a strong password.

Step 2: Identity Verification

- Upload a valid government-issued ID such as an Aadhaar card, PAN card, or passport.
- Ensure that the document is clear and legible to avoid delays.
- Some platforms may require you to submit a selfie or a live video for additional verification.

Step 3: Address Verification

- Provide proof of address using documents like utility bills, bank statements, or Aadhaar.
- Ensure the address matches the one mentioned in your ID document.

Step 4: Risk Assessment

- Some platforms may ask you to fill out a questionnaire about your income sources, occupation, and trading experience.
- This step helps the platform categorize users based on risk profiles.

Step 5: Approval

- After submitting all documents, the platform's compliance team reviews your application.
- The verification process may take a few hours to a couple of days, depending on the platform.

A flowchart depicting the KYC process, from registration to approval.

Challenges and Criticisms of KYC in Crypto

1. Privacy Concerns

Critics argue that KYC compromises user privacy by requiring personal information. Decentralization advocates believe that KYC conflicts with the anonymous nature of blockchain technology.

2. Lengthy Processes

Some users find the KYC process time-consuming, especially during periods of high demand on popular platforms.

3. Exclusion of the Unbanked

KYC often requires users to have government-issued IDs or bank accounts, which may exclude individuals in rural or underserved areas.

4. Data Breaches

The collection of sensitive data during KYC raises concerns about potential hacks and breaches. Ensuring robust cybersecurity measures is crucial.

How KYC Benefits Crypto Users

1. Safer Trading Environment

By verifying user identities, platforms create a safer environment for buying, selling, and holding cryptocurrencies.

2. Access to Advanced Features

Many platforms restrict access to features such as higher withdrawal limits, futures trading, and staking for non-KYC users.

3. Enhanced Recovery Options

In case of account hacking or loss of credentials, KYC-verified accounts have better chances of recovery through identity proof.

4. Participation in Global Markets

KYC compliance enables users to access global crypto services and participate in Initial Coin Offerings (ICOs) and other investment opportunities.

KYC and the Indian Crypto Ecosystem

1. Government Initiatives

The Indian government's emphasis on transparency in financial systems aligns with the adoption of KYC in crypto.

2. Emerging Platforms

Many Indian exchanges prioritize KYC to attract users and comply with RBI guidelines, fostering a more secure ecosystem.

3. Regulatory Developments

Stay updated with crypto-related announcements from the Ministry of Finance and the RBI to understand how regulations may impact KYC requirements.

A map of India highlighting major crypto adoption hubs and platforms implementing KYC.

Tips for Completing KYC Smoothly

1. **Ensure Document Accuracy** Double-check the details on your ID and proof of address to avoid rejections.
2. **Use Trusted Platforms** Choose platforms with a strong reputation for security and compliance.
3. **Be Patient** Verification may take time, especially during peak trading periods. Plan your investments accordingly.

4. **Secure Your Data** Avoid sharing personal information with unverified sources or platforms.

Real-Life Scenarios: KYC in Action

1. **Ramesh's Smooth Onboarding:** Ramesh, a tech professional, completed his KYC in under 24 hours using his Aadhaar card and started investing in Bitcoin.
2. **Priya's Security Lesson:** Priya initially hesitated to complete KYC but later realized its importance after a phishing attack on a non-KYC platform.
3. **Sunita's International Investment:** Sunita, a freelancer, used a KYC-verified platform to access global crypto markets and diversify her portfolio.

A success story visual showing a user's journey from KYC to successful crypto investments.

Conclusion: The Future of KYC in Crypto

KYC is an indispensable part of the cryptocurrency world, balancing the need for security and transparency with user accessibility. While challenges remain, ongoing technological advancements and regulatory clarity promise to make the process smoother and more secure. For Indian crypto enthusiasts, embracing KYC is a step toward building trust, enhancing safety, and unlocking the full potential of digital assets.

A futuristic illustration showing the integration of KYC and blockchain for a secure crypto future.

XII

Reader's Summary

Reader Summary of Why Crypto: Entry-Level Understandings of How Crypto Can Help You Achieve Your Dreams

This book, Why Crypto, is your gateway to understanding the transformative world of cryptocurrency. Tailored for Indian working professionals, freelancers, and dreamers seeking passive income, it demystifies crypto and explains how it can help you realize your aspirations.

1. **Introduction to the Crypto Revolution:** Discover why cryptocurrency is reshaping global finance and why it's particularly significant for India. Gain a brief yet compelling overview of the history of money and the rise of digital currencies.
2. **Crypto Basics for Beginners:** Get a solid foundation in cryptocurrency concepts, from understanding blockchain technology to exploring major currencies like Bitcoin and Ethereum.
3. **Setting Up Your First Crypto Wallet:** Learn step-by-step how to choose, set up, and secure a crypto wallet for your assets.
4. **Trading and Investing in Crypto:** Uncover the essentials of trading and investing, including strategies to mitigate risks and maximize returns.
5. **Crypto as a Passive Income Source:** Explore various ways to earn passive income through staking, lending, and yield farming.
6. **Real-Life Use Cases of Cryptocurrency:** Dive into practical applications of crypto in areas like remittances, e-commerce, and digital payments in India.
7. **Navigating Crypto Risks:** Understand common pitfalls, from market volatility to scams, and learn how to protect yourself.

8. **Legal and Tax Implications in India:** Stay updated on crypto regulations and taxation to ensure compliance and avoid penalties.
9. **The Future of Cryptocurrency:** Speculate on emerging trends and the role India might play in the global crypto ecosystem.
10. **KYC and the Role of Compliance:** Realize the significance of Know Your Customer (KYC) processes in building trust, security, and compliance in the crypto world.
11. **Empowering Your Dreams with Crypto:** Conclude with actionable steps and a mindset shift to leverage cryptocurrency in achieving your financial and personal goals.

Why Crypto provides a clear, relatable, and practical roadmap for Indian audiences who are curious yet cautious about entering the cryptocurrency space. Whether you're looking to start small or aim big, this book equips you with the knowledge to begin your crypto journey confidently.

GRATITUDE

As we come to the conclusion of *Why Crypto*, I hope this book has demystified the world of cryptocurrency and inspired you to explore its vast potential. While this journey marks the end of these pages, it is just the beginning for you—a new chapter in your financial and personal growth.

In this end matter, you will find additional resources, glossary terms, and references to ensure that you continue learning and growing in your crypto journey.

Glossary

- **Blockchain:** A decentralized digital ledger that records transactions across multiple computers.
- **Cryptocurrency:** A digital or virtual currency secured by cryptography.
- **Wallet:** A digital tool that allows you to store and manage cryptocurrencies.
- **Staking:** The process of locking up cryptocurrency to support a blockchain network and earn rewards.
- **KYC (Know Your Customer):** A process used by financial institutions to verify the identity of their clients.

References

This section includes a curated list of articles, websites, and tools that helped shape the content of this book and can further support your crypto journey.

1. Government of India on Cryptocurrency Regulation
2. Understanding Blockchain Technology
3. Leading Global Crypto Platforms
4. Basics of Trading

Acknowledging the Reader

To you, the reader, I extend my sincerest thanks. Your curiosity and commitment to learning are the catalysts for innovation and progress. By taking the time to explore cryptocurrency, you are positioning yourself at the forefront of a financial revolution.

Remember, the crypto world is dynamic and ever-evolving. Stay informed, stay cautious, and most importantly, stay curious. Your journey doesn't end here; it's only beginning.

With best wishes,

Jithender Kumar R

jk.lifecoachss@gmail.com

84838 99907

www.ingramcontent.com/pod-product-compliance
Lightning Source LLC
LaVergne TN
LVHW091116150826
845673LV00002B/849

* 9 7 9 8 8 9 6 7 3 2 6 5 5 *